BATMAN BEGINS

**Screenplay by
Christopher Nolan and David S. Goyer**

Story by David S. Goyer

Batman created by Bob Kane

LEVEL 2

SCHOLASTIC

***Batman Begins* adapted by:** Jane Revell

Commissioning Editor: Jacquie Bloese

Editor: Jane Rollason

Cover layout: Emily Spencer

Designer: Victoria Wren

Picture research: Emma Bree

Photo credits: Page 51: Imagesource; Imagestate; Image 100.

BATMAN, DC Logo, and all related names,
characters and elements are trademarks of
DC Comics © 2005.

WB Logo: TM & © Warner Bros. Entertainment, Inc.
Images courtesy of Warner Bros.

Published by Scholastic Ltd. 2005.

No part of this publication may be reproduced in whole or
in part, or stored in a retrieval system, or transmitted in any
form or by any means, electronic, mechanical, photocopying,
recording or otherwise, without written permission of the
publisher. For information regarding permission write to:
Mary Glasgow Magazines (Scholastic UK Ltd.)
Euston House
24 Eversholt Street
London NW1 1DB

All rights reserved.

Printed in Singapore. Reprinted in 2008.
This edition printed in 2009.

CONTENTS	PAGE
Batman Begins	**4–45**
People and places	**4**
Chapter 1: The blue flower	**6**
Chapter 2: Bats everywhere	**13**
Chapter 3: A man of the night	**19**
Chapter 4: The white smoke	**24**
Chapter 5: 'Rā's al Ghūl is dead'	**29**
Chapter 6: A surprise guest	**34**
Chapter 7: CRRAAASSSSHHHHH! ! !	**39**
Fact Files	**46–51**
Batman FAQs	**46**
Batman's gadgets	**48**
Facing our fears	**50**
Self-Study Activities	**52–55**
New words!	**56**

PEOPLE AND PLACES

BATMAN

The good guys

Batman

Batman's real name is Bruce Wayne. His home is Gotham Ci[ty]. Bruce comes from a rich family. They built most of Gotham City. The family home is called Way[ne] Manor.

Alfred Pennyworth has always worked for the Wayne family. He worked for Bruce's father and now he works for Bruce. He cooks, drives and takes care of everything.

Sergeant James Gordon is a police officer with the Gotham City Police Department.

Lucius Fox works at Wayne Enterprises in the Applied Sciences office. They think of new ideas here.

Rachel Dawes has [been] friends with Bruce [since] they were children. Her mother worked [at] Wayne Manor. Now Rachel is an Assista[nt] District Attorney in Gotham - that's an important lawyer - she wants to fight [the] bad guys.

BEGINS

The bad guys

Ducard is Number 2 to Rā's al Ghūl.

William Earle is the boss of Wayne Enterprises.

Crane is the most important doctor Arkham Asylum in Gotham City. The asylum is for people with mental problems. They put criminals here too.

Carmine Falcone is Gotham's biggest criminal. He gives money to important people and they follow his orders.

Rā's al Ghūl is a brilliant fighter with big ideas. He teaches Ninjas. He lives on a mountain in Bhutan in the middle of Asia.

Places

Gotham City was once a big, happy place. People had good jobs and busy lives. When this story begins, it is a dark and frightening city. Most of the important people are criminals. Nobody cares about the ordinary people.

Wayne Manor is a lovely, old house in Gotham full of expensive things. It has beautiful gardens. The Wayne family have always lived here. But there is only Bruce now and he is away. Wayne Manor is empty, except for Alfred.

Wayne Tower is in the centre of Gotham City. Wayne Enterprises and the train station are here.

Batman Begins

CHAPTER 1
THE BLUE FLOWER

Bruce Wayne was in prison in Bhutan, a country far away from his home in Gotham City in America.

One day, he was waiting for breakfast with all the other prisoners. They stood in lines. After a long time, Bruce got his plate of horrible food. He took the plate and walked to a table. A very big man stood in front of him.

'Give me your food,' said the man.

'No,' Bruce said.

The man hit Bruce in the face. Bruce dropped his plate and fell to the floor. When he got up, there were seven big men in front of him. Two of them took Bruce by the arms. He used his legs – hard – and they fell. Then –

CRRAAACCCCK!

At the sound of the gun, all the prisoners quickly got down on the floor. A prison officer took Bruce's arm.

'You're coming with me,' he said.
'Why?' asked Bruce. 'So I'm safe?'
'No,' said the officer. 'So *they're* safe!'

The officer pushed Bruce into a room and closed the door with a bang. It was very dark in the room, but Bruce saw that he was not alone. There was a man in the corner. He didn't look like a prisoner. He wore good clothes.

'My name is Ducard,' he said. 'I work for Rā's al Ghūl. Do you know him?'

'Is he a criminal?' Bruce asked.

'He is not a criminal,' said Ducard. 'He is a great man with very clever ideas. He knows that you're in trouble, Mr Wayne. He wants to help you.'

Ducard walked to the door and shouted. The officer came and opened it. Ducard turned to Bruce.

'There is a very special flower,' he said. 'It grows on the mountain near here. It's blue. Find it and take it to the top of the mountain. There you will find the answer to your question.'

'And what is my question?' asked Bruce.

'"Where am I going?"' said Ducard. And he left.

'Why is Ducard interested in me? How does he know about me?' Bruce asked himself. He sat on the hard bed and began to think about his life. He remembered that terrible day in Gotham many years ago.

He is a little boy. He is playing with his friend, Rachel. They are running in the garden at his home, Wayne Manor. There is an old well in the garden. Bruce climbs onto the well and laughs.
'Look at me, Rachel, I'm –'

Suddenly he isn't laughing. He's shouting.
'Help! Help! I'm falling –'
And he falls down and down and down into the dark well.
He hits the floor with a bang!
'Agh! My leg!' he cries. It feels terrible.
Then he hears some strange sounds. He isn't alone in the well! Help! What is it? He looks up and sees a cloud of terrible black things. Bats! They are flying towards him and into him. Their teeth are like knives. He thinks he is going to die. He makes himself into a ball and shouts. 'Help! Help!' Then everything goes black.

The next thing he remembers … he is in bed.
The only person in the bedroom with him is Alfred. Alfred has always worked for the Wayne family.
'You had a very bad fall, Master Bruce,' says Alfred. 'But you're going to be OK.' Alfred waits for a moment, then he asks, 'Why do we fall, Master Bruce?'
Bruce knows the answer, but he can't remember it.
'I can't remember,' says Bruce. 'Tell me.'
'We fall,' says Alfred with a smile, 'so that we can learn to get up again.'

Bruce started to climb the mountain. He found the blue flower easily. He climbed higher. Up and up he went. It got colder and colder. Soon he was walking on ice. It started to snow heavily. Bruce was cold and unhappy. And very tired.

'I have to get to the top,' he thought, 'but I don't know if I can.'

Then at last he saw a big building. He pushed open the heavy door and went in.

Rā's al Ghūl was sitting in a big chair. Ducard was next to him. And there was a line of Ninjas with swords in their hands … ready to fight.

Bruce was frightened. He quickly showed them the blue flower in his hand. Ducard took the flower.

'Are you ready to start?' he asked.

'Ready? Oh no,' Bruce said, 'I'm so tired.'

Ducard threw him to the floor. 'You must always be ready,' he said. 'Here we will teach you to be ready.'

One day, Ducard said to Bruce, 'You're not frightened of me, are you, Bruce? What *are* you frightened of?'

'Bats,' answered Bruce, and he told Ducard about the bats in the well. 'My father told me something important about the bats in the well.' He said, "The bats flew at you because they were frightened of you. All things are frightened of something, even scary things like bats." I didn't know that. My father was very clever. I loved him very much. But soon after that, he died. A criminal killed both my parents. His name was Joe Chill.'

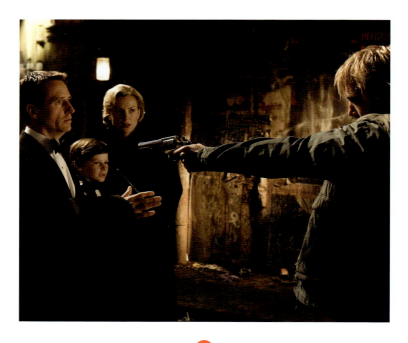

*It's the evening. They are at a play. Suddenly there are bats in the show. They fly around above the singers and dancers. Bruce is frightened, so they leave early. But in the street outside, there is a man with a gun. He wants money. He takes their money but he wants more. And then – **BANG!** – he fires his gun. Bruce's mother shouts. Bruce's father falls to the floor. **BANG**! He fires again. Bruce's mother falls to the floor. This is the worst moment of Bruce's life. And it is all his fault.*

'It wasn't your fault, Bruce,' said Ducard. 'You were very young.'

He was giving Bruce a lesson on a river. It was thick ice. They were fighting with swords.

'You must always look very carefully at the things around you, Bruce,' said Ducard. Suddenly he hit the ice with his sword.

CRRAAACCCCK!

The ice broke and Bruce crashed into the black water below.

Bruce had lessons with Ducard for many months. He learned to fight with his hands and his feet. He learned to fight with a sword and climb tall buildings quickly and quietly. He learned many things. But most of all he learned to use his ears and eyes, and he learned how to think quickly.

'It's time to test you,' said Ducard one day. 'Today you must fight all the Ninjas.'

So Bruce fought all the Ninjas with his sword. It was a very long fight, but in the end he won.

'You fight very well now,' said Ducard. 'I think you are ready.'

CHAPTER 2
BATS EVERYWHERE

Bruce couldn't sleep that night. He remembered his life after Joe Chill killed his parents. He was so unhappy and so angry. He went from school to school and university to university. He never stayed long in one place.

Bruce is twenty. He is going back to Gotham by train. Alfred meets him at the station. On the way to Wayne Manor he sees that everything is different. Everywhere is dirty. Many houses are empty. Many shops are closed. People are sleeping on the streets.

'Things are very bad in Gotham now, Master Bruce,' Alfred tells him. 'But Wayne Manor is still your home. Your father was a great man, and one day you will be a great man too.'

It is the afternoon on the same day. Bruce is sitting on his bed. 'Joe Chill will be free today,' he thinks. 'He killed my parents twelve years ago. And today I'm going to kill him.' He takes a gun out of his bag.

His old friend, Rachel, comes to the house. She is an Assistant District Attorney – an important lawyer in Gotham now. 'Wow!' he thinks when he sees her. 'She is so beautiful.' They drive to the prison.

'Why are they freeing Joe Chill today?' he asks.

'When he was in prison, he was in a room with Carmine Falcone, the famous criminal,' Rachel explains. 'They talked and he learned lots of things about Falcone. He's going to give that information to the police.'

They arrive outside the prison. The newspaper people are waiting. Joe Chill comes out. There are police all around him. Bruce gets out of Rachel's car and walks towards Chill. He has his hand in his pocket … on his gun.

But – suddenly – a blonde woman pushes through the people. She runs up to Chill. She has a gun in her hand.
'Falcone says "Hi, Joe",' she shouts. **BANG! BANG!** *She kills Joe Chill.*

Joe Chill was dead. But Bruce didn't feel better. It wasn't the answer.

Ducard took Bruce's blue flower. He pulled the dry flower into little pieces and made a small fire with it.

'Smell your flower now,' he said to Bruce.

Bruce put his nose near the smoke. The smell was terrible. He suddenly started to remember the worst days of his life … He was falling down the well … He was seeing his parents' blood in the street …

'You are frightened of these things. Look at them. Fight them. Now!' said Ducard.

He pointed to a large wooden box. Bruce opened it.
WHOOOOSSSH!

Hundreds of bats flew out of the box. Bruce wanted to shout and run. But he didn't.

'No,' he thought, 'I must be strong.'

He stood there quietly. He didn't move. He didn't say a word.

'Well done!' said Rā's al Ghūl. 'You are not frightened now. You are ready to join my Ninjas.'

He gave Bruce a light. 'Take this light and give your life to me.'

Bruce took the light. 'Where must I go with your men?' he asked.

'To Gotham,' answered Rā's al Ghūl. 'Gotham must die. You must kill all the people there.'

'No!' shouted Bruce. This could not be real.

'We have taught you many things,' said Rā's al Ghūl. 'Now you must do this for us.'

'I won't do it!' shouted Bruce. He threw the light on the wooden floor. It broke. A fire started and moved quickly around the room. It grew and grew. It reached the boxes of explosives in the cupboards. They started to explode.

BANG! BANG!

Ninjas ran everywhere. The roof started to fall. It fell on Rā's al Ghūl and killed him. As Bruce ran to the door, he saw Ducard's body on the floor. He wasn't dead. Bruce pulled Ducard out of the building and into the snow.

He pulled him down the icy mountain. Ducard was very heavy. Once he almost fell over the edge of the mountain, but Bruce saved him.

After some time they came to some houses. Bruce left Ducard with an old man there.

'You saved his life. I will tell him,' said the old man. 'Where are you going?'

'I'm going home,' said Bruce.

Bruce walked down the rest of the mountain. He phoned Alfred.

'I need you, Alfred,' he said. 'Please come and get me.'

Alfred flew to Bhutan in the Wayne family plane and took Bruce back to Gotham. He told Bruce all about the terrible changes in Gotham. Carmine Falcone was the crime boss in the city now. Everyone was frightened of him. And William Earle sat in Bruce's father's chair at Wayne Enterprises, the Wayne family business in Wayne Tower.

'Bruce Wayne is dead,' Earle told everyone. 'I'm the boss now.'

Bruce listened carefully to Alfred.

'I'm going to save Gotham, Alfred,' he said.

When they arrived home at Wayne Manor, Bruce saw a small black thing high on the wall.

'What's that, Alfred?' he asked.

'It's a bat, sir,' answered Alfred. 'There are lots of bats around here.'

Bruce suddenly ran out of the house. He ran to the well in the garden and climbed down and down. He reached the floor. It was very dark but he could feel a cold wind. He found a hole in the wall and climbed through. He could hear water. It was quite near. He followed the black walls until they opened into a big cave. A river ran

through the cave. And everywhere there were bats –
hundreds and hundreds of bats.

Bruce smiled.

The next morning Bruce put on a new suit and went to
Wayne Tower.

The woman at the front desk at Wayne Enterprises tried
to stop him. 'You can't go in there,' she said. 'They're
having a business meeting.'

But Bruce opened the door and went in. There were a
lot of men sitting around a long table. And at the end of
the table was William Earle.

'Good morning, Mr Earle. Good morning, everyone,'
said Bruce.

Earle's face went white but he quickly tried to smile.

'My boy! How nice to see you!' he said. 'You're back.
What a surprise! A *nice* surprise!'

'I've come back to work here,' said Bruce. 'I want to
learn the family business.'

Bruce started work in the Applied Sciences office. This was the new ideas office, but Wayne Enterprises didn't seem to be very interested in new ideas these days. The only other person in the office was Lucius Fox. Lucius was a friend of Bruce's father, before he died.

Bruce looked around the big room. It was full of strange and exciting things.

'What's this?' he asked, and pointed to a black suit.

'It's a body suit,' said Lucius. 'It can stop a knife. It can even stop a gun.'

'Can I have it?' asked Bruce.

'Of course,' said Lucius. 'All these things are yours anyway.'

Bruce took the body suit home and down to the cave. 'Soon,' he thought, 'I will be ready.'

CHAPTER 3
A MAN OF THE NIGHT

The night his parents died, Bruce waited a long time at the police station. One of the police officers there was very kind to him. His name was Sergeant James Gordon. Bruce knew that he was a good police officer. He wanted to talk to Gordon now.

But he didn't go as Bruce. He put on his black body suit and a mask.

When Batman appeared in Gordon's office, the sergeant was surprised and frightened.

'Who are you?' he asked. 'What do you want?'

'Don't be frightened, Sergeant Gordon,' said Batman. 'I need your help. I know Carmine Falcone is the biggest criminal in Gotham. Why is everyone frightened of him? Why does no one stop him?'

'Because …' said Gordon, 'he pays all the important people in Gotham!'

Bruce went to the river for the first time in many years. There were lots of people there. They didn't have homes. They slept in the streets every night.

Some people were standing around a fire. Bruce stood with them and warmed his hands. He looked across the street and pointed to a door.

'Is that Carmine Falcone's club?' he asked.

'Yeah,' someone said.

The next day at work, Lucius Fox said, 'Come with me, Mr Wayne. I want to show you something.'

Bruce followed him into a big room. There, in the centre

of the room, was a fantastic car.

A few moments later, they were in the car and Bruce was driving it faster and faster along the road.

'Go slower, Mr Wayne!' shouted Lucius.

'No way!' shouted Bruce. 'This is fantastic! This isn't an ordinary car. It's more like a plane. Can I have it?'

'Of course,' shouted Lucius. 'All these things are yours anyway!'

Later Bruce drove the car back to Wayne Manor. 'I'll call it the Batmobile,' he told Alfred.

Bruce was a man of the night now. He was Batman.

He stood on top of a building near Falcone's club. He watched the street by the river. He saw a police officer talking to a group of ship workers. The officer took out a small white bag and gave it to the workers. Drugs! So some of the Gotham police were bad too. Falcone was paying everyone.

Falcone sat in his office with Dr Crane, the boss of Arkham Asylum for the mentally ill.

'Our boss is arriving very soon,' said Crane. 'When I tell him about the money – *his* money – he won't be happy.'

'Don't tell him,' said Falcone. 'I won't take any more. This is the last time.'

He gave Crane a small bag.

'Do you want to test the drugs now?' he asked.

Suddenly there was a loud bang and the sound of guns. Crane quickly escaped through the door. Batman flew into the room.

'What *are* you?' asked Falcone.

'I'm Batman. Everything changes tonight.'

Batman crossed the city to Rachel's house. He climbed through her bedroom window. 'Rachel, wake up!' he said. 'I want to tell you something. Everything changes tonight!'

'And who are you?'

'A friend. I want to do good, like you. I want to fight the bad people of Gotham.'

Sergeant Gordon arrived at the river. A lot of newspaper people were there. They were taking photos. Next to a ship there was a large box full of small bags of drugs. Falcone's men were lying behind the box.

'Fantastic!' said Gordon. 'Where's Falcone? He always escapes trouble.'

'Not this time. Look. He's over there,' someone said.

Gordon looked. There was a big light next to the river. A man was lying across the light. He wasn't moving. It was Falcone.

Rachel read the newspaper the next day and saw the photo of Falcone on the front page. She smiled.

At the police station, Sergeant Gordon's boss was very angry.

'Who did this to Falcone?' he shouted. 'Find him fast! The police look stupid because of him.'

'I think he's trying to help us, sir,' Gordon said.

'We don't need his help!' shouted his boss.

'Well, I think we probably do,' thought Gordon. But he didn't say anything.

Dr Crane was visiting Falcone at the police station.

'Tell the police I'm mentally ill,' Falcone said to him, 'or I'll tell them about you and the drugs.'

Crane was angry. 'What do you know about me and the drugs?' he asked.

'I know that you test them on people in your hospital,' said Falcone. 'I know the boss is planning something big.'

'Would you like to see my mask?' said Dr Crane suddenly. 'I use it in my tests. People are very frightened of it. They don't like it at all.'

He opened his bag and took out a horrible mask. He put it on.

'How do I look?'

WHOOOOSSSH!!

Suddenly white smoke came out of his bag.

Falcone tried to shout but his nose and his mouth were on fire. Water came out of his eyes. He saw horrible things in front of his eyes. Crane quickly put the mask back in his bag and shut it.

He called a police officer.

'I think Mr Falcone is certainly mentally ill,' he said to the officer. 'We'll move Mr Falcone to Arkham Asylum. We can take care of him there.'

Earle was angry. Bruce Wayne was back in Gotham. Earle wanted to sell Wayne Enterprises for a lot of money, but now he couldn't.

And now he had another problem. His Number 2 at Wayne Enterprises, Rogers, was telling him about it.

'One of our biggest ships has disappeared,' said Rogers.

'There's a big, expensive machine on that ship,' said Earle. 'A very dangerous machine that can change water into steam.'

CHAPTER 4
THE WHITE SMOKE

'No one must know that I am Batman,' thought Bruce. 'Everyone must think that I am just rich and lazy.'

So one evening, Bruce went to have dinner at Gotham's most expensive hotel restaurant. He took two beautiful women with him, one on each arm. After dinner, the women wanted to swim in the hotel swimming pool.

'It's closed,' said the waiter.

'Then I will buy this hotel and open the swimming pool!' said Bruce. He jumped into the pool with the two women.

Later, when Bruce was leaving the hotel with the two women, he suddenly saw Rachel. She wore a fantastic dress and looked beautiful. She was just going into the restaurant.

'You haven't changed much, have you, Bruce?' she said. 'It's all fun and no work for you, isn't it?'

'Hey, Rachel. This isn't the real me.'

'The things you do are important, Bruce, not the things you say.' And she walked away.

Batman went to see Sergeant Gordon.

'There was someone in Falcone's office with him that night,' he said. 'He was testing the drugs. Do you know who it was?'

'No, I don't,' answered Gordon. 'Dr Crane from Arkham Asylum often visits Falcone. Perhaps it was him.'

'Yes, perhaps it was,' said Batman. 'I think I'll go to Arkham Asylum.'

'It's not safe,' said Gordon. 'It's in the Narrows, a very dangerous part of Gotham.'

'Not for me,' said Batman.

Batman soon arrived at the Narrows. Behind Arkham Asylum was a dark building. Batman went inside and found a very big ship's box. It was difficult to open. At last he was able to push open the top. Inside there was a machine – it was the size of a big car. Batman read the words on the box: 'WAYNE ENTERPRISES 47B1-ME'.

Two people came into the building. One was a ship worker. The other was a man in a dark suit. They didn't see Batman.

'What are the boss's orders?' asked the man in the dark suit.

'We keep the machine

here until he's ready,' said the ship worker.

'Fine,' said the man in the dark suit. It was Dr Crane.

Batman suddenly flew from the box to the floor.

'No, it isn't fine,' he said. He hit the ship worker in the face and he fell to the floor. Crane quickly put on his mask, and then he waved his arm at Batman.

WHOOOOSSSSSSHH

A cloud of white smoke came out of his coat.

Batman's nose and mouth were suddenly on fire. He started to see all the worst things from his life in front of his eyes.

'I've felt this way before,' he thought. 'But where?'

Then he remembered – Rā's al Ghūl, the wooden box, the bats, the building on fire …

He got to the window on his hands and feet.

Crane watched him. 'You're going to die, Batman,' he said.

Batman climbed slowly through the window, up the wall and onto the roof.

He pulled out his mobile phone.

'Alfred,' he said. 'Alfred, I–I need you. Please come quickly. I'm ill. And I need a blood test.'

Terrible thoughts were now in Bruce's head. He was at the show … the bats … his parents … a gun … blood in the street …

And then – nothing.

He opened his eyes. He was home, in his bedroom. Alfred came in.

'How long have I been asleep?' Bruce asked.

'Two days, sir,' answered Alfred. 'It's your birthday today.'

'It was the white smoke,' said Bruce. 'Luckily there

wasn't very much of it. But I've felt like that once before in my life. On the mountain in Bhutan. But this time it seemed much stronger.'

'I've got the results of the blood test,' said Alfred. He gave Bruce a piece of paper.

'It's a very dangerous drug,' he said. 'It can kill people. But I know someone who can make an antidote.'

The next day, Bruce showed the results to Lucius Fox.

'This was in your blood?!' he said. 'You're lucky you didn't die!'

'Yes, I've been very lucky,' said Bruce. 'Can you make an antidote?'

'I think so,' said Fox, 'but it won't be easy.'

'One more thing,' said Bruce. 'Do you know what Wayne Enterprises 47B1-ME is?'

'No, I don't,' said Fox. 'But I can probably find out.'

Sergeant Gordon went to see Rachel.

'Will Falcone go to prison this time?' he asked her.

'I think so,' said Rachel. 'It's in all the newspapers.'

'Batman came to see me, Miss Dawes,' said Gordon. 'He asked for my help.'

'Yes, I know,' said Rachel. 'He came to see me too. We're working with a man in a mask, Sergeant Gordon. Perhaps he's dangerous.'

'I don't think so,' said Gordon. 'He's done lots of good things already.'

The door opened and Bruce Wayne came in.

'Oh sorry,' he said. 'I'll come back later.'

Gordon knew Bruce Wayne from the newspapers.

'It's OK, Mr Wayne,' he said. 'I was just leaving.' He

went out.

'What do you want, Bruce?' Rachel asked angrily.

'I want to invite you to a party tonight,' he said. 'And to say I'm sorry.'

Rachel smiled. She could never be really cross with him. 'Where's the party?'

'It's at home – at Wayne Manor,' he said.

An officer opened the door.

'They've moved Falcone from the police station to Arkham Asylum,' he said.

'Who decided that?' asked Rachel.

'The boss there, Dr Crane.'

Rachel quickly put some things into a bag.

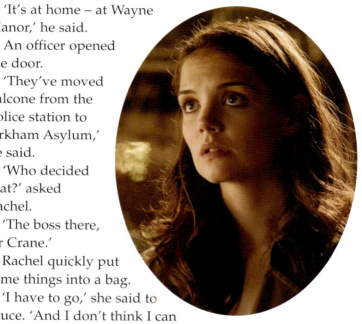

'I have to go,' she said to Bruce. 'And I don't think I can come to your party tonight. I'm sorry.'

She opened the door and turned to Bruce.

'Happy Birthday, Bruce!' she said.

CHAPTER 5
'RĀ'S AL GHŪL IS DEAD'

Rachel was in Dr Crane's office at the asylum.

Batman was listening outside the building.

'Falcone is just going to prison when he suddenly becomes mentally ill,' said Rachel. 'Isn't that a little strange, Dr Crane?'

'Would you like to see Falcone, Miss Dawes? Then you'll be able to decide for yourself,' said Crane. 'Come with me. I'll show you.'

Falcone lay on his bed. He couldn't move.

'Mask … mask … mask …' he was saying.

'You've given him drugs!' said Rachel.

'Yes, of course.' said Crane. 'We give drugs to all our people here. It's a hospital!'

'The police doctor must see him and do some blood tests,' said Rachel. 'I'm going to call him right now.'

'Very well,' said Crane. 'Come this way.'

They went down some stairs and came to a door. It had an electronic lock. Crane put some numbers in and it opened. They turned right and walked to a large room. There were hundreds of small blue bags on the tables. People in white coats were working at the tables.

'We make our drugs here,' said Crane.

Rachel turned and ran. She got to the door, but Crane had locked it again. She pushed different numbers. Nothing happened.

Suddenly a horrible masked man appeared next to her … and then a cloud of white smoke …

Rachel lay on a table.

'Who knows you're here?' shouted Crane. 'I want to know before I kill you.'

'What do we do now?' asked one of the men.

'Call the police,' said Crane.

'You want the police here?' asked the other man. He was surprised.

'Batman's here,' said Crane. 'I'm sure of it. The police will catch him.'

Suddenly a black thing flew at them and hit the two men. They fell to the floor.

Batman looked around. Where was Crane? He heard a sound behind him and turned. In the dark he saw a mask and a hand. Batman pulled the mask off Crane's face. He held Crane's hand under his own nose. Smoke came from a bottle inside Crane's coat. White smoke.

WHOOOOOOSSSSSSH!

Crane's body dropped to the floor.

'Who are you working for?' shouted Batman. 'Who's your boss?'

'Ra's ... Rā's al Ghūl,' said Crane. He spoke with great difficulty.

'Rā's al Ghūl is dead, Crane,' said Batman. 'Who are you really working for?'

Crane's eyes closed. He said only a few words. 'Mask ... drugs ... smoke ... water ... steam ...'

There was a loud voice outside.

'Batman, come out. There are police everywhere. We are all around the building. You can't escape.'

Batman found Rachel. He took her in his arms and climbed up to the roof.

Sergeant Gordon went into the building to find Batman. He started to climb the stairs. Suddenly he felt an arm around him and he was flying up and up.

Batman dropped him carefully onto the roof.

Then Gordon saw Rachel lying there.

'What's happened to her?' he asked.

'Crane gave her a dangerous drug,' said Batman. 'She'll die very soon. I must get the antidote for her.'

'How will you escape?' asked Gordon.

'I'm going to call for help,' said Batman.

He pushed something on his shoe – it made a very high sound.

A big, black cloud started to grow in the sky above Gotham. It grew and grew and moved nearer and nearer. Finally it came down on the hospital roof.

Bats! Thousands of bats!

They flew all around Bruce and Rachel. The bats hid Batman and Rachel until they reached the Batmobile. Batman drove home to the Batcave. When they arrived, Bruce looked at Rachel carefully. Her eyes were closed and she wasn't moving. She was cold. He carried her from the Batmobile to the worktable. He gave her the antidote. He hoped that it wasn't too late.

At Arkham Asylum there were police everywhere.

A young police officer ran over to Sergeant Gordon.

'Sir!' he shouted. 'There's something that you must see.'

Gordon followed him into another big room. In the centre of the floor was a small door. It was open.

Gordon looked through the door and saw the river below. There were five or six large bottles next to the door.

'They've used the river for something,' said Gordon, 'but what?'

He looked at the bottles.

'I want to speak to someone at the Water Office,' he shouted. 'Now!'

Rachel woke up. She felt terrible.

'How do you feel?' someone asked. She knew the voice. She looked at the face. It was Batman!

'Where am I?' she asked. 'Why did you bring me here?'

'You were very ill,' he said. 'I rescued you.'

'I remember now. That horrible mask,' she said. 'It was Crane. I must tell Sergeant Gordon.'

She tried to move.

'No, don't get up. Stay where you are,' said Batman. 'Sergeant Gordon has got Crane already.'

'Why did you save my life?' she asked.

'Gotham needs you,' he said. 'Here, take this. It will help you sleep. When you wake up, please find Sergeant Gordon. Give him these.'

He held up two small bottles. 'Only Gordon. No one else.'

'What are they?' she asked.

'The antidote to this killer drug,' said Batman. 'One bottle is for Gordon himself. He can use the other bottle to make some more of the antidote for everyone.'

'Crane wasn't the boss. He was working for someone else,' Rachel said. 'Something al Ghūl.'

'Rā's al Ghūl,' said Batman. 'No, it's not Rā's al Ghūl. He's dead. I was there when he died.'

But Rachel was asleep.

CHAPTER 6
A SURPRISE GUEST

In the empty workroom, Sergeant Gordon was talking on the phone.

'Someone has put a dangerous drug into the city's water,' Gordon said.

'Well, we test the water every day,' answered the man from the Water Office, 'and today's results seem fine.'

'Perhaps it's safe to drink but dangerous to smell,' said Gordon.

'That's possible,' said the water man.

When he finished his phone call, Gordon saw the large ship's box.

'What's that?' he asked. 'Let's open it.' They got the top off and found a machine.

'It's bigger than a car,' said an officer. 'What does it say on it?'

'WAYNE ENTERPRISES 47B1-ME,' Gordon read.

'What does it do?' asked an officer.

'I've no idea,' answered Gordon. 'But no one must go near it. OK?'

Bruce left the cave and went up into the house. Everyone was having a great time at his birthday party. When he appeared, they all sang 'Happy Birthday to you!'

Bruce walked around saying hello to his guests. Finally he found the person he wanted. Lucius Fox.

'That machine – ' he said quietly, 'Have you found out anything?'

'Yes, I have. It can change water into steam,' Fox said.

Bruce thought for a moment. 'So you could put a dangerous drug in the water,' he said. 'And then you

could change the water into
steam and kill everyone in
the city. Could you?'

'Yes, you could,' said
Fox.

'Oh no!' Bruce went
quietly across the room
towards the door. He had
to leave as soon as possible.
But on the way, a woman
took his arm. It was Mrs
Delane, an old friend of his
father.

'Bruce!' she said. 'I want
you to meet someone.'

'I'm sorry. I can't stop now, Mrs Delane,' said Bruce. 'I
have to ...'

But then he looked at the man with Mrs Delane. The
man wore a blue flower in his jacket.

'This is Mr al Ghūl, Bruce,' said Mrs Delane.

'You're not Rā's al Ghūl,' Bruce said to the man.

'No, you're right, Bruce,' said a voice behind him.

He turned around. It was Ducard.

'He isn't Rā's al Ghūl,' said 'Ducard'. 'I am. I'm not
Ducard. I never was. And you, Bruce, were my best
student until you escaped.'

Bruce looked around the room and saw that he didn't
know some of the people there. They weren't his friends.
They were Ninjas!

His guests were in danger. They had to get out fast.
What could he do? He took a glass and shouted, 'Let's
drink to my birthday! Let's drink to all my guests! You
don't like me, do you? You're here because you like my
money. You just want some free food and drink!'

The guests were very upset and angry. They left the house at once. They got in their cars and drove away.

Rā's al Ghūl laughed. 'They will die very soon anyway,' he said.

'So was Crane working for you?' asked Bruce.

'Yes, he was,' said Rā's al Ghūl. 'But he was only interested in money. I want much more than that. When Gotham dies, people everywhere will be frightened. There will be fighting and killing all over the world. Man will disappear. No more people. The world will be wonderful again. I saved you, Bruce, but you fought me. You set fire to my home. Since then your activities have made trouble for us. Now we're going to make trouble for you.'

Rā's al Ghūl shouted an order to his men, 'Go ahead!'

The Ninjas started to set fire to the furniture.

Some kilometres away at Arkham Asylum, four police officers were standing around the machine.

'What did Gordon say? "No one must go near it,"' one of them said. 'Except us, of course.' They all laughed. Another one looked at his watch. 'It's time,' he said.

They turned on the machine and then put explosives along the wall.

They weren't following Sergeant Gordon's orders.

At the same time, high above the city, a train driver looked at his watch.

'The train stops here,' he said. 'Everyone out!'

The passengers got out. The same thing was happening on buses and trains all over the city. Everything in Gotham stopped.

Sergeant Gordon was standing outside Arkham Asylum.

Rachel ran towards him. She gave him the two small bottles. 'These are from Batman.'

FOOOOM!

Before he could answer, there was a big explosion. Gordon ran towards the room with the machine. There was no wall. Four police officers were pushing the machine outside. One of them pushed something on the machine. It started to make a strange sound.

FOOOOM!

There was a second explosion.

FOOOOM!

Then another.

FOOOOM!

Then another.

There was steam everywhere. A small cloud of steam moved towards Gordon. The smell reached him. His nose and mouth were on fire.

At the Water Office, the workers were looking at a map of Gotham City. There were small lights all over the map. All the lights were green. Except one. The light at Arkham Asylum was red.

Wayne Manor was on fire.

'Have you come to kill me?' Bruce asked Rā's.

'No,' said Rā's. 'I've come to ask you a question. Will you join us?'

'Never!' said Bruce. 'I don't want to be part of this.'

'Then fight me,' said Rā's, 'and die with Gotham.'
He took out a sword.

They fought and fought until finally Bruce stood over Ra's with his sword above Rā's head.

'You taught me very well, Rā's,' he said.

'Yes, I did,' said Rā's, 'but you always forget to look very carefully at the things around you.'

CRRRAAACCCK!

Bruce looked up. The roof was on fire. Part of it was falling towards him.

BANG!

It hit him and he fell to the floor.

'Goodbye, my friend,' said Ra's. He ran out of the building. A car was waiting for him.

CHAPTER 7
CRRAAASSSSHHHHH!!!!

'Master Bruce! Master Bruce! Get up!'

Bruce opened his eyes. Alfred was next to him. And a part of the roof lay on top of him.

'Push!' said Alfred. 'You're strong. You can do it.'

Bruce pushed and pushed, and finally Alfred moved the piece of roof to one side. Bruce got up and they escaped to the cave below.

'Oh, Alfred,' he said. 'What have I done? Wayne Manor is on fire and I can't help Gotham. I've made so many mistakes.'

Alfred smiled. 'And why do we fall, sir?' he asked.

'We fall,' said Bruce, 'so that we can learn to get up again. I must go!'

He changed into his Batsuit and took off in the Batmobile.

FFFWHOOOOSSSHH!

In a few minutes he was in Gotham.

The criminals from Arkham Asylum were running everywhere. They were shouting and dancing and breaking things. Rachel watched. Above her a train stopped. Some men in masks started to move a large machine onto it.

She ran to find Sergeant Gordon in the asylum. He was sitting on the floor. She could see that he was very ill. He needed the antidote fast. She took one of the bottles out of his pocket.

'It's OK,' she said. 'I can help you.'

Rachel gave Gordon the antidote and he slowly started to feel better. The people from the asylum were shouting and coming nearer. They were feeling bad from the white cloud. Suddenly they started running towards Rachel and Gordon.

'Oh no!' thought Rachel. 'They're going to kill us.'

WHOMMMM!

The Batmobile arrived from nowhere. Batman ran towards Rachel. He gave Gordon the keys to the Batmobile.

'Drive carefully,' he said. Batman took Rachel in his arms and climbed up to the roof with her – above the dangerous cloud. Gordon ran to the Batmobile.

From the roof Rachel and Batman could see all of Gotham.

'They were putting a large machine onto the train,' said Rachel.

Just then, the train started to move. Batman suddenly understood.

'Of course,' he said. 'The railway line runs exactly over

the river next to Wayne Tower. Rā's is going to use the machine there. He's going to turn the city's water into steam. He's going to kill everyone.'

Batman moved to the edge of the roof.

'Batman, don't jump!' said Rachel. 'You could die. Please tell me your name.'

'The things I do are important, not the things I say.'

'Bruce? ... Bruce!' shouted Rachel.

But Batman couldn't hear. He was flying down. He landed on the roof of the train and held on.

BANG! BANG! BANG! People inside the train fired guns through the roof. They hit Batman three times. He fell off the roof.

The Ninjas in the last car of the train looked out of the window. First they looked up. No Batman. Then they looked down. Batman was still there! He was hanging from a long line, flying from side to side under the train.

On a street below the train, there was a Ninja in the back of a green car. He was pointing his machine gun at Batman. Gordon came around the corner in the Batmobile. He was driving very fast.

KERZAMMM!!

He hit the green car. It crashed and exploded into a ball of fire.

Batman climbed up the line to the train. He got into the last car and finished the Ninjas there. Then he went to the front of the train.

When he reached the first car, Rā's turned. His mouth opened.

'You!?!' he said. He took out his sword and ran at Batman.

Batman quickly moved to the front edge of the train. Ra's lifted his sword over Batman's head. Batman held it and broke it in two.

The train was moving nearer and nearer to the centre of Gotham. It was moving nearer and nearer to Wayne Tower.

'I must stop the train,' thought Batman.

He reached out of the front of the train and threw Rā's al Ghūl's sword under the wheels. There was a terrible noise.

Rā's threw himself onto Batman and put his hands over his mouth and nose. Batman couldn't move. Everything started to go black.

'Now you're really frightened, aren't you?' said Rā's.

Batman looked into Rā's face. He saw the end of the world there. That made Batman angry. And when he was angry, he was strong. He suddenly pushed hard against Rā's and flew out of the train and into the sky.

Rā's looked up in surprise and anger. Then he was very frightened. The train was going to crash in less than a second. It came off the railway line and fell down and down. And then –

CRRAAASSSSHHHHH!!!!

It landed in the car park in front of Wayne Tower and exploded into a ball of fire.

Soon all the bad guys were in prison or out of a job. The people of Gotham began to build their great city again. Everyone wanted to work together now.

William Earle walked into his office the day after the train crash. He found Lucius Fox behind his desk.

'What are you doing in my office?' he asked.

'It's my office now,' said Fox happily. 'I'm the new boss of Wayne Enterprises.'

'Who says?' Earle asked.

'I say,' said Bruce from behind Earle. 'It's my business. Goodbye, Mr Earle.'

There were builders at Wayne Manor. They were slowly and carefully building a new house – exactly like the old one.

Bruce went to the old well in the garden. He put a big piece of wood across the top. Rachel was there with him.

'I fell down this well a long time ago. Do you remember?' he asked her.

'Of course,' she answered.

'Things were never the same after that,' he said.

'What was different?' she asked.

Bruce put another piece of wood across the well. Now it was completely closed.

'I wasn't a child anymore, he said. 'I began to be a man.'

'You're a great man, Bruce,' she said.

Bruce looked at her. She could see that he loved her.

'There's no place for me between Batman and Bruce Wayne,' she said.

'I don't have to be Batman,' he said. 'I can choose my own life.'

'No,' she said. 'I don't think you can. Great people can't always choose their lives. Gotham needs you. Goodbye, Bruce.'

'Goodbye, Rachel,' he said. 'I'll do my best for Gotham.'

'I know you will,' she said.

FACT FILE

BATMAN

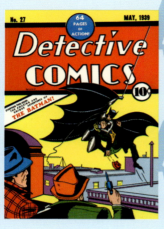

When did Batman first appear?

Batman is one of the world's most famous comic heroes, and he's been around for a while – over 60 years in fact! He first appeared in *Detective Comics* #27 in 1939.

Does Batman have special powers?

No. Batman isn't like Superman or Wonder Woman. He's an ordinary person like you or me. He can't fly, he can't walk on water and he can't climb buildings by himself.

Q So, how does Batman always win the fight against crime?

Because he has learned to do some very clever things. He's a brilliant detective and he's very good at martial arts. He fights well and thinks quickly. He's also very good at escaping. And he's got some very special gadgets (see next page!).

Find out what these words mean: comic hero   power   martial arts   gadget

ICE LINE DO NOT CROSS   POLICE LI

FAQs

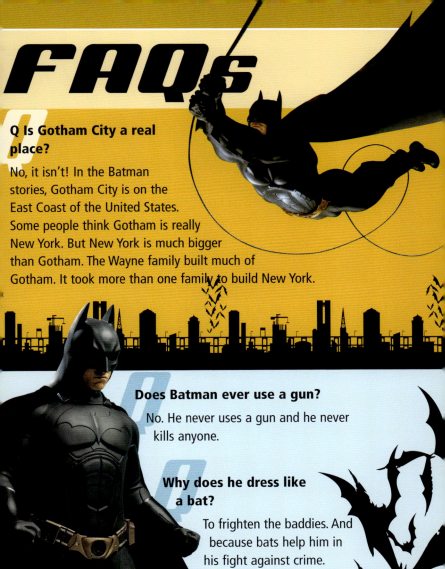

Q Is Gotham City a real place?

No, it isn't! In the Batman stories, Gotham City is on the East Coast of the United States. Some people think Gotham is really New York. But New York is much bigger than Gotham. The Wayne family built much of Gotham. It took more than one family to build New York.

Does Batman ever use a gun?

No. He never uses a gun and he never kills anyone.

Why does he dress like a bat?

To frighten the baddies. And because bats help him in his fight against crime.

> Work in pairs. Make a list of all the comic heroes that you know. What nationality are they? Who's your favourite comic hero? Why?

FACT FILE

BATMAN'S GADGETS

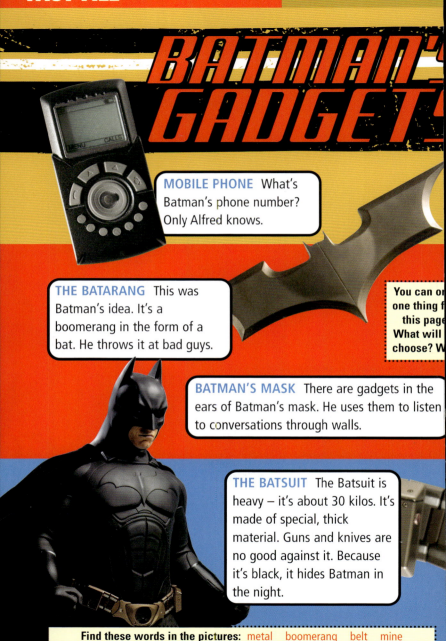

MOBILE PHONE What's Batman's phone number? Only Alfred knows.

THE BATARANG This was Batman's idea. It's a boomerang in the form of a bat. He throws it at bad guys.

You can o
one thing f
this pag
What will
choose? W

BATMAN'S MASK There are gadgets in the ears of Batman's mask. He uses them to listen to conversations through walls.

THE BATSUIT The Batsuit is heavy – it's about 30 kilos. It's made of special, thick material. Guns and knives are no good against it. Because it's black, it hides Batman in the night.

Find these words in the pictures: metal   boomerang   belt   mine

THE BATMOBILE The Batmobile is a cross between a Lamborghini Countach and a Humvee, first called the Tumbler. It can jump across a river.

Has Batman got everything he needs? Make a new gadget for him.

THE BATCAVE is below Wayne Manor. Main floor: Batman's **COMPUTER** is here as well as his Batsuits. Lower floor: Batman keeps the **BATMOBILE** here.

THE UTILITY BELT There is a very strong wire on this belt. It's very long too. Batman joins one end of the wire to the roof of a high building. He holds the other end and drops down to the ground.

MINI MINES Batman uses these to blow things up.

What do these words mean? material wire

FACT FILE

Facing our

"I was frightened of bats. I'm not now. I know they're frightened of me!"

In *Batman Begins*, Bruce Wayne faces his fears and becomes a much stronger person.

NOOOO! IT'S SCARY!!!

Being frightened is sometimes a good thing. It teaches us about life. We are frightened of things as soon as we are born. Babies don't like loud noises. And they don't like their mum disappearing.

It teaches us to look out for danger. Before we walk into a dark room, we think, 'Is it safe? Am I frightened?'

> **A teen magazine asked 1,000 British teenagers: 'What are you most afraid of?'**

Here are their top six answers. (Use a dictionary if you need to.)

1. global warming
2. falling from a high place
3. car accidents
4. ghosts
5. bullies
6. spiders

> **Do you agree with them? What frightens you?**

Fears

We can be frightened of...

...things around us

'I hate being high up. I hate being on top of a building or a mountain. I don't even like going up in a lift!' **Jemma, 15**

'A dog jumped up and pushed me over when I was three. I've been frightened of them ever since.' **Max, 12**

...people around us

'I'm worried my girlfriend will dump me. I don't think I'm good-looking or funny enough for her.'
Fred, 14

'I don't like parties. I think, "I won't know anyone. No one will talk to me. And if they do, I won't know what to say!"' **Tara, 14**

'I know it's stupid … but … I'm really frightened of standing in front of the class. If the teacher asks me to come to the front, I just die inside.'
Ashley, 14

...things in our heads

'I'm afraid of ghosts!'
Dean, 13

What do these words mean?
fear   dump   global warming
bullies   spiders

Work in pairs. Give advice to the people above. What could they do to face their fears?

SELF-STUDY ACTIVITIES

Chapters 1-2

Before you read
Use your dictionary for this section.

1 Use these words to answer the questions.
bat   cave   ice   roof   suit   sword
Which
   a) is big and cold?
   b) is hard and cold?
   c) is something you wear?
   d) is dangerous?
   e) is an animal that flies at night?
   f) is on top of a house?

2 Which is which?
   tower   well
   a) A … goes up a long way.
   b) A … goes down a long way.

3 Find the best word for each definition.
   begin   exploding   hole   mental
   a) If you have one of these in your pocket, your money falls out.
   b) When something goes bang and breaks into pieces, it is doing this.
   c) You do this kind of work in your head.
   d) You do this to a book when you open it at page one.

4 Use these words to complete these sentences.
   prison   criminal   lawyer
   a) The … said, 'This man took the money from the bank.'
   b) The … said, 'I didn't do it. I was as at home watching TV.'
   c) They sent the … to … .

5 Look at People and Places on pages 4-5.
   a) Who do you think will win - the good guys or the bad guys?
   b) Something happens to Wayne Manor in this story. What do you think it will be?

After you read

6 Answer these questions.
- **a)** How does Bruce get out of prison, do you think?
- **b)** Why is Bruce afraid of bats?
- **c)** What happens to Bruce's parents when they leave the play?
- **d)** What are the most important things that Ducard teaches Bruce?
- **e)** Why doesn't Bruce kill Joe Chill?
- **f)** What happens when Bruce smells the smoke of the blue flower?
- **g)** What kills Rā's al Ghūl?
- **h)** Is William Earle pleased to see Bruce?

7 What do you think?
- **a)** At the end of Chapter 2, Bruce says, 'Soon I will be ready.' What will he be ready for?
- **b)** Who will be a friend to Bruce – Lucius Fox or William Earle?

Chapters 3-5

Before you read

8 Choose the right word for each definition. Use your dictionary.
antidote   drugs   machine   mask   steam
- **a)** We use these to wash our clothes and plates.
- **b)** If you take very hot water outside into cold air, this comes off the water.
- **c)** People take these to get better.
- **d)** This hides your face.

Write a definition for the word you didn't use.

After you read

9 Bruce visits the people by the river. You live by the river. Write about your life now and ten years ago.

SELF-STUDY ACTIVITIES

10 Answer these questions.
  a) Who works for who? Put these names in order:
  Dr Crane   Carmine Falcone   the ship workers   'the boss'
  b) Who put Falcone on the light at the river?
  c) Why does Dr Crane make Falcone take the drug in the police station?
  d) What two problems does William Earle have?

11 Put the right name in each space.
  a) … wants everyone to think that he is rich and lazy.
  b) … rescues Batman from Arkham Asylum.
  c) … is going to make an antidote to Crane's drug.
  d) … thinks Batman is a good guy.
  e) Bruce invites … to his party.

12 Put these events in order.
  a) Hundreds of bats help Batman and Rachel to escape.
  b) Batman gets onto the roof with Rachel.
  c) Batman makes Crane take his own drug.
  d) Crane give Rachel some of the drug.
  e) Dr Crane shows his drugs to Rachel.
  f) Rachel tries to escape.
  g) The police arrive and they want Batman.

Chapters 6-7

Before you read
13 What do you think?
  a) Dr Crane says Rā's al Ghūl is his boss. Why does he say this?
  b) What have the bad guys done to the river?
  c) Chapter 6 is called 'A Surprise Guest'. Who will be the surprise guest at Bruce's birthday party?

After you read

14 Correct these sentences.
    a) The Water Office people have found a dangerous drug in the water.
    b) Lucius Fox doesn't know what the machine can do.
    c) Rā's al Ghūl is Ducard.
    d) Bruce says horrible things to his guests because he doesn't like them.
    e) Bruce sets fire to Wayne Manor.
    f) The roof of Wayne Manor falls on Rā's al Ghūl.
    g) Rā's al Ghūl doesn't escape.

15 Answer these questions.
    a) How does Rachel help Gordon?
    b) How is Rā's al Ghūl going to kill everyone in Gotham?
    c) Why don't the Ninja guns kill Batman?
    d) The train doesn't crash into Wayne Tower. How does Batman stop it?
    e) Who is boss of Wayne Enterprises now?
    f) Is Rachel going to marry Bruce?

16 You work for the Gotham City newspaper. It is the day after Rā's al Ghūl came to Gotham with the Ninjas. Write a headline for the newspaper.

17 Answer these questions.
    a) How does Rachel find out that Bruce Wayne and Batman are the same person? Look at pages 24 and 41.
    b) Why does Rā's al Ghūl want to kill all the people in Gotham, do you think?

New Words!

What do these words mean?

antidote (n) ....

bat (n) ....

begin (v) ....

cave (n) ....

criminal (n) ..../crime (n) ....

drug (n) ....

explode (v) ..../explosive (n) ..../

explosion (n) ....

hole (n) ....

ice (n) ....

lawyer (n) ....

machine (n) ....

mask (n) ....

mental (adj) (hospital) ..../

mentally (adj) ill ....

prison (n) ....

roof (n) ....

steam (n) ....

suit (n) ....

sword (n) ....

tower (n) ....

well (n) ....